Introverts Guide To Conve
How To Go From Shy To Social in an
Extroverts World

By Makram Shakur

Disclaimer

Table of Contents

Introduction

I would like to personally thank you and congratulate you for taking the first step to gaining communication skills by downloading my book, *"Introverts Guide To Conversation."*

Through reading the *"Introverts Guide To Conversation"*, you will gain an inside view of exactly how to communicate like an extrovert. Additionally, you will be able to quickly learn the basic ideas of communication as well as how to implement them, regardless of your individual introvert limitations to conversing in a social environment.

Introversion is neither negative nor positive; it is simply a factor of personality types. It has mutually positive and negative impacts, learning to acknowledge and accept both of them will ease the transition of learning to flourish within any conversation.

Once again, thank you for choosing to download this book. I sincerely hope it provides the knowledge and help that you have been searching for.

Understanding Introvert Communication Characteristics

Whether you are an introvert or an extrovert comes down to simple personality traits. People often look at introversion in a negative light, whereas in actuality, there are several qualities to introversion that can be seen as positive personality traits. Unfortunately, being an introvert can often make it seem as if you are trapped in an extrovert world. In many ways you are as most people are extroverts. This is why there are some real advantages to stepping out of your introvert shell and picking up a few extrovert characteristics. Doing so can dramatically change your life and help you achieve your personal and professional goals.

There are five main types of introvert characteristics. You may fall into one type or have characteristics similar to a few. To determine the type of introvert traits that constitutes your personality, consider the basis of each type.

Lack of Gregariousness - The Loner Effect

Gregariousness is a simple quality of truly enjoying being around others. The lack of gregariousness, however, is enjoying complete alone time, free from the interactions of others. Extroverts look at this personality trait as if there were some type of deep flaw. They fail to understand that most introverts who prefer alone time, thrive off of their own inner thoughts. They have a tendency to think in a deeper and often philosophical way.

If a lack of gregariousness happens to be a factor guiding your personality, you will more than likely experience the love for a good book and enjoyment of being completely alone in your room. Additionally, you may also experience times of deep contemplation, thorough problems solving everyday issues, and from time to time, you may allow yourself to come up with innovative design theories that could alter the future. These are all good qualities that are only limited by the potential inability to take the next step of expressing your thoughts and ideas.

The inability to expand, combined with the societal perspective of introverts, can lead to negative coping skills. If you have not nurtured your introversion, while simultaneously actively gaining a little extroversion, you may have negative reactions. There are good chances that at least at some point you have lashed out, been lead by frustration or even withdrawn to an even deeper internal place.

Activity Avoidance - Staying on the Sidelines

Introverts with activity avoidance have a great deal of difficulty blending into an extrovert society. Activity avoidance can vary in severity. You may avoid all activities or you may go out with friends only to stay tucked away in the corner, safe from too much interaction.

As an introvert that avoids activity, you are most likely rather laid back. This helps you to avoid confrontation. However, it can also prevent you from gaining interpersonal skills and you will find it difficult to build relationships and advance in your career. As you can imagine, this type of introvert trait can have negative impacts.

By learning to accept that your need to avoid social events is not a character flaw, and that it is simply a personality trait, you will be able to move forward. You will be able to begin building strategies that will allow you to become comfortable in social events, thereby improving back and forth communication. This in turn, with time and practice, will help to provide comfort in social environments.

Lack of Positive Expression - Mimicking Monotone Traits

Lack of positive expression as an introvert can effect several areas of life. You may experience limited friendships, awkward professional moments and heartbreaking relationships. The outward effect towards extroverts, who may not understand, may lead to several negative impacts in your own life. You may experience sadness as friends and would be loved ones separate from you all a result of their misconception that you do not care.

Learning to include a splash of extrovert personality traits can help teach you how to show your inner emotions. With a little determination and practice you will be able to allow others to see and experience how much you care. This also can improve working conditions as employers begin to see you as a passionate employee who is concerned with the wellbeing of the company and others around them.

In many ways, a lack of expression can lead to several life disappointments as career paths become stagnant, friends move on and love is lost. For this reason, learning to express thoughts and feelings at a comfortable pace can ensure a productive and enjoyable life, free from regrets.

Limited Assertiveness - Overly Polite, Considered Shy

A commonly recognized character trait of an introvert is the inability to show assertiveness. This is often looked at as an abundance of shyness. Rather than speaking up, an introvert would rather be polite. Whereas politeness is usually a positive trait, in the case of an introvert, it can be damaging.

While being ultra polite, many introverts are failing to ask for the things that they want and need. Learning to speak up can definitely help in such a case, but it does take a little practice. Once skills have been learned, standing up for oneself becomes easier.

The politeness factor of shyness is simply a coping skill. Rather than stating that something is not all right, it is accepted within a polite tone. If this sounds familiar, you are more than likely taking on several responsibilities that you do not desire. Unfortunately, though a politeness coping skill, the average extrovert does not realize there is a problem. An extrovert typically will not acknowledge a problem on their own, you will have to actually speak up and tell them. Failing to do so will result in the continuous feeling of being taken advantage of. Enlisting communication skills will provide an alternative to automatic acceptance at the cost of your inner happiness.

Minimal Drive for Adventure - Peace and Quiet Seekers

A key characteristic of introverts that comes from a simple low adventure drive is the desire to play it safe. Typically, introverts will avoid adrenaline based activities. However, events that would seem adventurous to an extrovert will also be passed by, as this trait leads to an introvert who simply needs to thrive within their own individual world of quiet peace.

An aversion to adventure personality trait can in fact be lessened. It is often as simple as slow self-reinforcement. By actively participating in small adventurous activities you will be able to expand upon your physical and social world.

This process is actually quite easy. By implementing the communication strategies within this guide, you will gain confidence within a crowd. In turn, you will be willing to include yourself in many social events, thereby placing yourself in a position to actively take part in an adventure. This may not necessarily come easy; however, it certainly will not be impossible either.

In actuality, as confidence is built you may surprise yourself when you discover that you were able to enjoy a summer ball game. You may even be able to finally experience those elaborate winter parades, right along with the crowd. As you continue to try out new things with the friends you were never really able to appreciate, your fear of risk will diminish, thereby providing you with a life that you may have never believed was truly possible.

The Path to Learning Communication Tactics

Learning how to communicate confidently and freely, as an introvert, can be a difficult task. However, it can be accomplished with minimal difficulty. All you will need is a willingness to expand beyond your comfort zone as well as a commitment to diligently practice these introvert communication tactics.

A willingness to take on communication barriers is necessary when developing new communication tactics. You will need to accept the challenges that will eventually provide communication comfort. This can be scary at first; after all, you will literally be dropping your introvert safety net and immersing yourself into an extrovert environment. Fortunately, each time you accept a new communication challenge you will gain strength through conquering past obstacles.

Through continual practice, you will gain comfort. You will learn to blend into any communication style. Practice will allow you to make light conversation through small talk, a key to any sized social event.

As you become more comfortable speaking in small and large groups, your dedication level will increase.

This is a natural course, for every success leads to a desire to achieve more. Even as an introvert, you can reach a point of competitive desire. You will discover an internal competitiveness to successfully communicate in any surrounding. This will drive your determination.

Determine Your Specific Introvert Personality Trait

Since introvert characteristics are different in individual personalities, it is imperative that you determine exactly what makes you an introvert. Are you uncomfortable around others? Do you find that you need to fully evaluate a topic, prior to speaking?

Introvert Traits

Social Aversion

People often look at an introvert's aversion to social interactions as rudeness, and at times they may even refer to the person as being stuck up. In actuality, quite the opposite is true. Often they will like each person within the group, though on a single platform.

Introverts may even become overwhelmed within a large group. This is not so much that they dislike the people within the group; it simply comes down to a need for less interaction. Keeping this in mind as you learn communication tactics will help you understand your individual social difficulties.

You have probably at some point experienced a feeling of being overwhelmed within a large group. You may even feel awkward within a group. This can cause insecurity within yourself. By remembering that you are completely self-reliant and overly independent, you will be able to place false beliefs behind you.

Your fear of social encounters is merely a fact of your personality traits; however, it does not have to be a concrete factor. You can practice communication styles within social events, both personal and professional. As you gain experience, communicating freely, you will be able to accept the social world around you. This will provide you with the opportunity to broaden your seemingly small world.

Delayed Processing

A misunderstood introvert sign is delayed processing. It stems from deeper thinking. While extroverts talk quickly and move from one topic to the next, an introvert has a tendency to fully digest each mentioned point within a conversation. Often, people who fail to grasp this concept will tend to believe that the introvert is not listening or that they lack understanding. The reality is that they have a higher level of understanding and they truly hang onto to every single word.

If you have the delayed processing personality trait you typically absorb all the information around you. This is an excellent trait to have although it is an aspect that can cause you to over-think in a conversation. Additionally, you may find it incredibly difficult to communicate with extroverts.

The typical extrovert conversation may cause an acceleration of frustration. This is primarily a result of the fact that you will want to continue a topic so that it can be fully explored and digested. Getting past this desire takes mental training.

You will need to learn how to quickly make mental notes on interesting aspects of the given topics. Doing so will allow you to further your interest when inside of your own environment. Unfortunately, you will rarely have the opportunity to stay within a deep conversation with an extrovert. On the rare occasions that you do, it is usually during one on one conversing, during relaxed downtime, and the extrovert may not be able to handle it. After all, they tend to get just as frustrated when they feel trapped into a long conversation that appears to have no end in sight.

Dislikes Small Talk

A struggle for many introverts is accepting small talk and taking part in small talk. It can be misleading as many extroverts, unknowingly, will assume that you lack interest or in general do not want to take part. In actuality, you more than likely can feel drained of energy after even a short time of attempting to take part in small talk. This can become a burden, especially during work-based gatherings. It can also create a difficult situation among friendships, especially among extroverts who thrive on small talk.

Through practicing small talk you will become comfortable in social situations. However, reaching a point of surviving small talk without feeling drained of energy will take time. Small talk is actually a conversation style that can easily be achieved through taking part in little doses of it. By minimizing the amount of time you face with communicating within this style you will be free to excuse yourself, thereby allowing yourself a short break.

Having the available space to take a few short breathers can dramatically recharge your internal batteries. This will prevent frustration and help you to keep from becoming overwhelmed. Furthermore, by providing the breaks that you need you will be better equipped to shine within a conversation when it matters most.

Accept Your Introvert Traits So that You Can Accept Change

A few all too common issues that can arise out of introvert traits is a feeling of awkwardness around others, loss of confidence and an overall uncertainty of social surroundings. These issues can be remedied through your own personal acceptance. Instead of fighting the traits of introversion, you should accept them as part of yourself. Through acceptance, you can recognize potential limitations and then begin to evolve.

Instead of concentrating on the negative aspects of introversion, look at what can be contributed. Considering the love of books that most introverts have, there should be an endless amount of available information that can be added into any conversation.

In fact, with practice, you should be able to eventually use your vast knowledge to start up one conversation after another.

You will also want to keep in mind that through accepting your introvert traits you will be able to see yourself in a new light. You will recognize your inner qualities as strengths. Once you have reached this point, the debilitating awkwardness that you have been plagued with will begin to fade.

Familiarize Yourself within a Social Climate

If you have a tendency to avoid social events you can easily overcome this by slowly becoming familiar with social encounter dynamics. Keep in mind that there are no expectations of your involvement. Extroverts will not be singling you out in your presence. With this in mind, start out by simply being a part of a social group. You do not need to be the life of the party.

Simply sit back and watch how each person reacts to each other. If someone is joking, smile casually. Most importantly, take in the environment and feel the energy. Realize first that there isn't any negative energy; the entire social group is simply enjoying themselves, albeit differently than how you have enjoyed your downtime throughout your entire life.

In the beginning, just start out slow with small two-hour events. As you become more comfortable, begin expanding with larger events. As you continue to immerse yourself into social crowds you will eventually become completely relaxed within a social environment.

Controlling a Delay in Processing

Delayed processing is an introvert trait that in actuality provides an immense advantage. Having this trait ensures deeper knowledge. Additionally, it prevents misunderstanding within a conversation. Unfortunately, while in the presence of a group of extroverts, following a conversation can be difficult, at best.

Extroverts are known for their ability to jump from topic to topic. The problem here is that while you are still processing the information that was just mentioned, they have already moved three topics over. It stands to reason that following this type of extroverted conversation can be a difficult task.

Next time you find yourself attempting to keep up with a conversation think back to your school days. Make mental notes with highlights on key points. Concentrate only on the primary points within a conversation. This will allow you to stay within a conversation in an extrovert crowd. To satisfy your need for deeper understanding, you can always sink into deep thought once you have returned to the sanctity of your quiet, still home.

The advantage here is that by exploring the discussion points in more detail you will be better prepared for future conversations. You will basically be giving yourself a near infinite pool of topics that can be accessed as needed. Extroverts may in fact view you as extremely informative and entertaining.

Learning the Art of Small Talk

Small talk is one of the most irritating conversation styles that introverts have to deal with. As an introvert, you more than likely find it exhausting and a bit pointless. Unfortunately, it is a feature of the extrovert world found within every social encounter. Therefore, learning how to deal with it and learning to take part in it can dramatically improve your ability to interact at work or while out in public and at those pesky family gatherings.

Before taking part in small talk, you will need to simply be a part of it. Listen closely to the extroverts around you and take note of the key points mentioned. Small talk has a great deal of advantages; it allows people to quickly grab tidbits about personalities and interests of the other people around them.

While you are examining extroverts involved in small talk, you will notice for some, it is as simple as mentioning the weather, a game or a recent movie. Others will expand even further by including a blurb on a recently read book. Yes, extroverts do read books! They may even quickly mention current events, recent medical reports or upcoming tech projects.

In all aspects, small talk allows a mass amount of individuals to discuss the world around them without having to take a great deal of time. Through small talk, people can quickly get the latest points on a topic of interest and continue on with their day. To an introvert, this conversational style can seem nearly impossible at first, though with practice it can be learned. Prepare for any occasion by considering your interest.

Prepare for social events by asking yourself a few questions

Have you recently read a new book?

What type of movies, TV shows or plays do you enjoy?

Has a recent news story intrigued you?

As you can see, small talk is made up of anything that interests you, combined with your personal likes and dislikes. Mentally replay your interests each morning and when the time comes you will not be standing around wondering what to say or how to respond.

For example, let's say you are at a get together and someone you do not know says that they recently saw the latest Men in Black movie. Your response could be something like this:

I haven't seen that yet, though I really think the last ones were funny. I especially liked the scene in the post office when Will Smith brought the Aliens to K's attention.

Just like that, you have actively taken part in small talk.

How to Effectively Begin a Conversation

Now that you have had some time to practice following a conversation and small talk, it's time to step it up a notch and start your own conversation. This can be nerve racking, especially with individuals that you are not comfortable with and those that you just do not really know that well. You can, however, gain confidence in starting a conversation through preparation and using targeted conversation starters.

Starting a conversation is as simple as, mentioning a hot newsworthy topic, an entertainment headline or inquiring about someone else's life. You will want to keep it simple though by sticking with questions regarding work, social circles or recent weekend getaways. Pay special attention to ensure that you do not delve too deep. Avoid topics regarding tragedies, politics and religion, as these topics are typically too personal for anyone other than a close friend.

Preparation for Your Next Opportunity to Converse

Aside from having plenty of topics in your mind, you will want to really spend a few moments simply relaxing. Keep in mind this is only a conversation. The worst that could happen is the possibility of starting a conversation with someone who you just don't share a general interest with. For greater assurance, you might want to practice among strangers that you will never see again. After all, if you never see them again then it just will not matter if you do not come off strong.

Through practicing with strangers you will discover firsthand just how easily conversations can begin. You will also be able to see for yourself that if one person is not all that approachable, there are several others that will be. This is a common feature within any social gathering as most people, being extroverts, will want to speak to anyone about almost anything. At the same time, be on the lookout for the people who would prefer to just sit back and enjoy people watching. It could just be that you are not the only introvert in the room.

Try out the following conversation starters, and watch as a conversation quickly comes to life.

At a party, business gathering or seminar with mostly strangers:

1. Comment on how great the party is.

2. Ask which company someone works for.

3. Ask about how well someone knows the host or guest of honor.

4. Mention a personal interest on a theme.

At any gathering with people you are familiar with, expand on day to day topics:

1. Ask what they thought about last night's episode of _____.

2. Mention a trending article online.

3. Ask about their weekend.

4. Mention someone who just got a promotion.

As a last resort, you can always refer to the basis of interpersonal small talk:

1. Mention the weather.

2. Compliment an outfit.

3. Comment on anything being served, food is always

a conversation starter.

4. Express enjoyment of your surroundings, i.e. "What a great party, they sure have chosen a good mixture of music."

How to Converse to Keep a Conversation Going

Conversing in a social environment can span far beyond small talk and the act of starting a conversation. The ability to keep a conversation naturally flowing is essential. It prevents that infamous awkward silence that everyone, extrovert and introvert alike, dreads.

In reality, the middle of the conversation is the most important; it's the core, the heart of all conversations. Without it, people would merely be mentioning odd pieces of information without substance. The ability to actually get to know anyone would be lost. For this reason, learning to expand on small talk with natural communication is essential to social success.

Open ended questions

The best way to keep the flow of conversation is to ask open-ended questions within the topic being discussed. In other words, be sure to ask questions that cannot be answered with a simple yes or no. Consider the two examples below and watch how the second example allows for conversation flow whereas the first allows for a stop.

Example 1

Question: I really enjoyed watching Identity Thief. Did you find it funny when Jason Bateman discovered the extent of how well she operated by stealing identities?

Answer: Absolutely, it was kind of funny.

Example 2

Question: I really enjoyed watching Identity Thief. Even though it was a comedy, it was rather amazing to see the extent of Diana's operation. Can you imagine someone actually pulling that off?

Answer: Yes, I liked it too. I believe it actually did mimic the problem with real life identity theft. Most of the people that steal the identities of others are professionals that have been surviving with it for years.

Example one allowed for a stop in communication. However, in the second example, the word imagine is used which allows for a moment of deeper thought. This opened up for a more in depth answer. Additionally, it provided an open for a topic switch. What began as a conversation about a recently watched movie merged into a topic based on common criminal and financial problems.

This is the essence that all good conversations are built of. What begins as a simple inquiry evolves into something more concrete. This transition may take place once or several times within any conversation.

How to Avoid Awkwardness when Leaving a Conversation

Leaving a conversation can be difficult for introverts. You might have had the experience of trying to leave a group conversation only to have an extrovert make a small joke about it at your expense. This is not meant to be mean, nor is it a matter of making fun of you. It's simply a result of the extroverts need to mention every single thing that takes place around them.

Another all too common situation, which introverts have to deal with when wanting to leave a conversation, is staying out of politeness or fear of ridicule. How many conversations have you painstakingly stayed in, simply to be polite? If you have stayed as a result of fear, you have probably noticed that the anxiety created was certainly as bad, if not worse, than the initial fear experienced.

There are lots of tricks for leaving a conversation. The ruin the conversation trick, where you turn the conversation into something so boring that people are fleeing from you, is one of them. Another is the famous, "Oh, hey! I promised my friend that I would save him/her if the sign was given." These can definitely work in a pinch although they can also backfire. The best policy is to remain as honest as possible.

By using honesty you might simply state, "It's been great talking with you, however, I do need to go mingle." Another option is to simply call it a night. Both of these are the main reasons that people leave conversations. Therefore, by using them, you are making a brief mention of something that has been heard over and over. As a result you will be excused without saying something that will make you stand out.

The other fact that you want to keep in mind is that extroverts rarely hang onto the reason someone left. They are typically already onto the next new thing within mere seconds of you leaving. In fact, short of announcing your departure at the top of your lungs, tripping on the way out the door or presenting a completely bizarre reason for leaving, you will escape as quietly as you entered.

How to Keep the Party Going, Even as an Introvert

Attending parties can be quite a challenge with the difficulties spanning far beyond holding and participating in a conversation. Since the traits of introvert personality types can cause frustration when overwhelmed and over-stimulated, an introvert can dramatically struggle during a party. This is the primary reason that most introverts have often avoided parties altogether.

However, through consistent practice, careful planning and purposeful moments of separation, parties can be quite enjoyable. You will notice that with each party you will be more relaxed, and in time you will even find yourself having fun. Parties are a great way to unwind, connect with old friends and enjoy the company of others.

Dealing with the Social Environment of a Party

During an average party, you will need to participate in a conversation while being surrounded by multiple other conversations that are going on around you. You will also possibly have your children and their friends running around behind you. This constant commotion can become overwhelming if you allow yourself to fall off guard.

Dependent on the type of party, you may also have the awareness of someone cooking on a BBQ and the music playing. If it is your party, you can expect an endless stream of interruptions from those asking questions and providing party compliments. All of these party based situations can be distracting and they can cause a slight panic if you are not careful.

In order to properly deal with the vibrancy of a party setting, you will need to maintain acute mind over matter control. Basically, you will need to acknowledge your surroundings and then push them to the side. Unfortunately, this is not a one-time fix. In fact, throughout the course of a party, you may need to regain mental control repeatedly.

If you experience an overwhelming drain of energy, no matter what you do, you may need a brief escape. Take just a moment and step into the solitude of the nearest restroom. Take this time to soak in the quietness, close your eyes, lean against the wall and feel yourself melt into the coolness of the restroom wall. Now open your eyes, take a deep breath and experience an energy renewal. With fresh energy, you are ready to join the party for another round.

Using Conversation Skills During a Party

During a party, social groups are consistently forming into circles only to break and form new circles. This can be distracting for an introvert. Not only will you need to participate in a typical social conversation, but you will also need to be consciously expanding from one circle to the next. This requires the ability to switch between topics, acknowledge new people and realize that the ones you were actively conversing with are swaying in and out of the conversation.

Often in a multi-conversational situation, one where a stream of people are consistently entering and leaving, small talk can be a lifesaver. It will allow you to converse without entering into long drawn out conversations that can leave you hanging as a group dissolves into another one. You will also want to keep in mind that you do not need to host every conversation. It is always all right to listen to newly forming conversational points and then simply reply to them once a new conversation is in flow.

Is it Possible for an Introvert to Communicate Professional Power?

The one thing that most people never associate with an introvert is power. Understandable, considering that power does not really line up with quietness, solitude and shyness. Nor does it seem in line with the overly polite or the ones that people do not really recognize. Instead, power is associated with boldness, risk taking and confidence. The traits that are associated with power are those of extroverts.

Power created through extrovert traits can in fact have a downside. Extroverts within a professional high stress environment can appear aggressive. They can inadvertently push people away, though sadly, they may never notice it. In a professional workplace that contains multiple demands, often it is the introvert that can display power. In fact an introvert can make an amazing leader built solely through respect.

Introvert Communication Styles that Lead to a Powerful Business Persona

A little politeness can go far in business. In fact, dependent on the industry, it can pull in new clients, move million dollar homes and build professional relationships. Unlike the extrovert that can appear aggressive, an introvert can seem open, honest and genuinely concerned.

These qualities can place potential clients and business partners at ease, leading to an increase in profits. Anytime that profits are up and a single person seems to be responsible a big percentage of the time, the company CEO's will take notice. This will ultimately lead to career advancement and an eventual high power position.

Retaining Power Possessed Through Introvert Traits

Gaining a powerful business reputation through accessing internal introvert traits, while simultaneously implementing learned communication skills, can be quite beneficial within the business world. However, once you have achieved this degree of power, you will need to retain it. One small slip up that points-out a lack of confidence or indecision can ruin all of your hard work and bring you crashing down.

In order to prevent a shift in power, you will want to continuously reinforce your communication skills while also feeding your introvert needs and desires. This can be achieved through spending a few hours of your day catching up on current events or diving into a great book. It will also require that you continue to converse at all given opportunities; at a chance meeting, in the store, or on a subway, bus or any other public transportation that you may choose to use.

Conversing with Ease by Putting it All Together

Knowing how to participate in small talk, taking part in any point within a conversation and leaving a conversation free of awkwardness can vastly expand an introvert's social circle. Staying relaxed at heavy social events can also help to ensure that the event does not become a theme of awkwardness. Furthermore, learning to utilize the positive introvert traits can certainly maximize your career outlook.

To really communicate effectively, you will need to properly combine the communication skills that you have learned. In a sense, you will need to master communication through becoming an expert with each aspect of communication. Only when you can put all of your learned communication skills together will you truly be able to blend within an extrovert world.

How Exactly Can You Communicate Effectively Within an Extrovert World?

Communicating effectively by following communication techniques will allow you to freely communicate within an extrovert world. This can be achieved through a great deal of practice, while also actively taking small steps. Furthermore, effective communication can be mastered through continuously taking part within social gatherings of all sizes.

How to Recover from Introvert Communication Pitfalls

Consider the fact that as an introvert, social communication does not come naturally. It is a skill that must be learned and practiced. With any skill that has to be learned, pitfalls can happen. This is a fact of life. The important thing though, is not to panic.

If you find yourself at a social event where you become overwhelmed and you shut down or suddenly blurt something out completely out of topic context, do not let this worry you. Instead smile, take a deep breath, and try to laugh it off. Always remember, that though you may not see it, everyone at some point has experienced similar situations. For this reason, people really will not dwell on your temporary lapse. That is, unless you choose to.

About The Author

Makram Shakur emigrated from Iran with his family when he was a young boy. His natural introversion caused him some difficulty in adjusting to his new land. Undaunted and with a great appreciation for the opportunities that America offered he applied himself to overcoming his shyness and general aversion to small talk. His experiences are the basis for this book.

One Last Thing

Thank you again for purchasing this book! I hope you found it useful!

The next step is to apply what you have learned. I know you can do it!

Finally, if you enjoyed this book would you be kind enough to leave a review for it on Amazon or wherever you purchased it from? It would be greatly appreciated!

Thank you and good luck!

22285095R00031

Printed in Poland
by Amazon Fulfillment
Poland Sp. z o.o., Wrocław